A Young Citizen's Guide To:

Money

Anna Davidson

HODDER
Wayland
An imprint of Hodder Children's Books

A Young Citizen's Guide series

Central Government
The Criminal Justice System
The Electoral System
The European Union
Local Government
The Media in Politics
Money
Parliament
Political Parties
Voluntary Groups

Published in Great Britain in 2002 by Hodder Wayland,
a division of Hodder Children's Books

Editor: Patience Coster
Design: Simon Borrough
Artwork: Stefan Chabluk
Picture research: Glass Onion Pictures
Consultant: Dr Stephen Coleman

British Library Cataloguing in Publication Data
Davidson, Anna
A young citizen's guide to money
1. Money - Great Britain - Juvenile literature
I. Title II. Money
332.4'941

ISBN 0 7502 4091 1

Printed and bound in Hong Kong

Hodder Children's Books,
a division of Hodder Headline
Limited, 338 Euston Road,
London NW1 3BH

Picture acknowledgements:
the publisher would like to thank the following for permission to use their pictures: AKG Photo 6 (bottom, AKG London/Erich Lessing), 13 (top, AKG London), 13 (bottom); The Bridgeman Art Library 6 (top), 7 (Bibliotheque Nationale, Paris), 10 (Guildhall Library, Corporation of London); Mary Evans Picture Library 8 (top); Hodder Wayland Picture Library 5, 9, 16; Impact 4 (Piers Cavendish), 11 (Mike McQueen), 14 (Piers Cavendish), 20-21 (Mike McQueen), 25 (Giles Barnard), 26 (top), 28 (Piers Cavendish); Popperfoto 8 (bottom), 19, 27; Popperfoto/Reuter 12, 23 (Chris Helgren); Topham/ImageWorks 22; Topham Picturepoint 17, 18, 24 and contents page, 26 (bottom), 29 and title page.

Cover: City workers at computers (Topham/ImageWorks); share prices on screen (Topham/PA); Euro bank notes (Topham Picturepoint); the Bank of England (Topham Picturepoint); UK bank notes (Topham Picturepoint).

Contents

What is Money?   4

Banks   10

Managing the National Economy   14

Global Finance   20

You and Your Money   25

Glossary   30

Resources   31

Index   32

What is Money?

Money, we are told, makes the world go round. Most people want more of it. A lot of people blame their problems on a lack of it. You might think money means pounds (£) and pence (p). In fact, that's not the whole story. Money is something you use to pay somebody else for goods or services that they provide. Because that person in turn might want to use what you give them to pay another person for something else later on, money needs to keep its value.

A £20 note in your pocket will have cost no more than three-and-a-half pence to produce. It is our law and custom that give this piece of paper its value, allowing it to be exchanged for £20 worth of goods or services.

A woman exchanges cash for goods at her local shop.

This sketch, by a member of explorer Captain Cook's crew, shows another crew member being offered a crayfish by one of the Maori people in return for a length of cloth.

Barter The first societies didn't have money, they used barter – swapping one thing for another. This meant that if one person grew vegetables while another raised chickens, they might exchange them, agreeing between themselves how many vegetables one chicken was worth.

This was not very efficient for lots of reasons. The vegetable grower might not have wanted any chickens but have been unable to find anyone who could give him something he did want before his vegetables went rotten. Or he might only have had enough for half a chicken – leaving the other person with the other half. And the two people bartering needed to be able to agree at the same time what both the chickens and the vegetables were worth.

Our money is much more convenient because it allows us to receive payment for something on one day and not spend it again until we want to. It also allows us to compare the value of products easily, because everything can be expressed neatly in pounds and pence. If a CD costs £15 and a magazine costs £1, it is easy to see that you could get fifteen magazines for the price of one CD.

The first money In any society that grew more sophisticated, with people producing less of their own wants – such as food and clothing – and trading more instead, the disadvantages of barter became overwhelming. Instead, goods, for example, shells, began to be used as money. As early as the thirteenth century BC, cowrie shells were given as gifts in China, and they were regularly used as small change in India up until the nineteenth century. Decorative strings of clam shells called 'wampum' were used in North America in the seventeenth century. Even up until the twentieth century, 'kina' shells were still being used in Papua New Guinea.

Cowrie shells, an early form of money.

Salt, tobacco, rice, cloth and dogs' teeth have all been used in different parts of the world as means of exchange. Precious metals, such as gold and silver, came to be adopted in many places because they had the advantages of being rare, so that they kept their value, and of being easy to divide up into coins of different standard sizes and weights. Controlling this process of supplying man-made money gave governments extra power.

The first coins were made in western Turkey in the seventh century BC. At about the same time, they were also being developed in China. In Britain, the first coins were made much later, around 80 BC, in south-east England. Today, coins are produced by the Royal Mint and are made of non-precious metals, such as copper, nickel and zinc.

An early coin, stamped with a ship and a mythical beast, probably dating from around the 4th century BC.

Paper money The earliest recorded use of paper money was in China in the seventh century. Its use did not become widespread in Europe until the seventeenth century. From the sixteenth century onwards, businessmen called goldsmith-bankers used to look after wealthy people's gold for them, to keep it safe. They would provide the owner with a hand-written receipt, promising to pay the person back on demand. The receipt, known as a 'running cash note', often also promised to pay the gold to whoever was in possession of the note – the bearer. This meant it could be passed around from one person to another, like a modern bank note.

In 1694 the Bank of England was established and, like the goldsmiths, it too started to issue notes in return for sums of money left in its care (deposits). Eventually, the 1844 Bank Charter Act gave this bank alone the right to issue notes in England and Wales. The Act also allowed the Bank of England to issue paper notes even if there wasn't actually the gold in store to back each one.

A painting showing how an early form of paper money, made from tree bark, was used by the Great Khan in thirteenth-century Mongolia.

Writing out and signing every bank note was a lot of work. In 1855, the first fully printed notes were issued, complete with the phrase: 'I promise to pay the bearer on demand the sum of…'. This still appears on modern notes, but you can no longer go along to the Bank and demand gold!

The Bank of England still prints notes for England and Wales today. In Scotland, three different banks issue Scottish notes, and in Northern Ireland four banks issue notes for use there. Scottish or Northern Irish notes are worth exactly the same as their English/Welsh equivalents. However, strictly speaking they are not 'legal tender', in other words under the law these particular notes could be refused by a creditor as settlement of a debt!

A printed bank note from the nineteenth century, with the words 'I promise to pay the bearer…'.

Paper money does not last long. A £5 note stays in circulation for about nine months – between February 2000 and February 2001, 240 million new ones were issued. Sorting machines at the banks separate out the notes that are too tatty to reissue. These are shredded – six tonnes are disposed of in this way every day.

The highest denomination note ever issued was the £1,000 note, ceased in 1943.

Modern money In the twenty-first century, cash – coins and notes – is still the most usual way to pay, but its use is decreasing. Cheques are being used less, too. Another, increasingly important, option is plastic cards. Issued by banks, they allow users to authorize the transfer

of money electronically between bank accounts. Most adults in the UK hold at least one of these cards, for example Visa, Switch or Delta.

Plastic cards are also used to withdraw three-quarters of all the cash in circulation, via automated teller machines (cash machines). In the future, we might see a new kind of money, to make buying and selling things over the internet (a process known as e-commerce) easier than using a plastic card and less open to fraud. It is likely that whichever company develops successful 'e-cash' will make a lot of money....

Credit and charge cards are popular types of plastic cards. There are around 45 million credit cards in use in the UK.

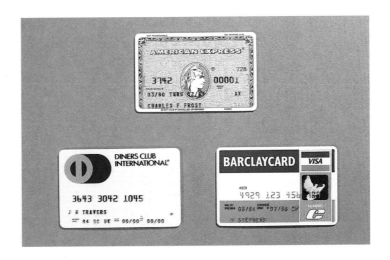

Forgery

A fake note is worth absolutely nothing. What's more, it's illegal to pass on or even to keep one. So it's in your interests to check that any note you receive is genuine. If you hold a note up to the light you should see the watermark (a faint design made in the paper during manufacture) – it shows a clearly defined portrait of the Queen. You should also see a bold, continuous line, which is in fact metallic thread embedded into the paper. These are two of the features of an authentic Bank of England note.

Instead of keeping wads of cash under the mattress or in a top drawer, the majority of adults in the UK today keep their money in a bank. Many also borrow money from a bank when making a big purchase like buying a house, or if they are running a business. There are several different types of banks, but they all have one thing in common. They link up people with spare money who want to put it aside for use in the future (savers) with people who need to spend money now but don't have enough of it readily available (borrowers).

The earliest bankers
Banking in England developed as recently as the seventeenth century. The goldsmiths decided that it made sense to use the gold sitting in their safes and lend it out at a price. To encourage savers to keep their gold with them, they would pay them. This was in addition to issuing notes (see page 7).

At the end of the century, King William III needed a huge amount of money to finance a war against France. The goldsmiths did not have enough to lend him. A Scottish merchant suggested that a bank be created to lend to the government and, in 1694, £1.2 million was lent by businessmen to set up the Bank of England.

The Great Hall of the Bank of England, 1809.

It soon became the biggest bank in the country, at the centre of a network of private banks in London, which had links with local banks in the country. Many more appeared in the second half of the eighteenth century. In the nineteenth century, large numbers of the private banks gave way to 'joint stock banks' which were owned by lots of people, not just one or two. Today these are known as commercial banks.

Commercial banks and building societies

The commercial banks in the high street such as Barclays, HSBC, Lloyds TSB and Royal Bank of Scotland all take deposits from the general public. When you put money into your 'account', the bank will lend it out again to somebody else. They might give you a regular payment, called interest, to encourage you to lend. The banks charge the people they lend your money to more interest than they are paying you, because they are in business to make a profit.

The exterior of the Bank of England today.

Building societies, such as Nationwide, were originally set up to help people save and borrow to buy or build a house. Instead of trying to make a profit, the idea was that any extra money earned would go towards giving the members of the society (the savers and borrowers) better deals. Over time, the building societies started to offer many banking services, such as cheque books and cash cards. There are now few building societies left, because many of their members have voted to convert them into banks altogether.

Investment banks

Investment, or merchant, banks do not do business with the general public. Instead, they bring together lenders and borrowers of very large sums of money. Their clients are mainly businesses and government departments. They also give advice (at a price!) to companies, on matters such as how to raise capital (money to run a business), buying or merging with other companies, selling off bits of a business, or floating on the stock exchange to become a public limited company (see page 22).

'…central bankers are not paid… to look on the bright side of things. We are paid to worry, to worry about what might go wrong and to anticipate the clouds coming over the horizon. We don't have to be particularly inventive to find plenty of work to do!'

Sir Edward George, governor of the Bank of England, in a speech to the Bankers' Club Annual Banquet at the Guildhall, London on 14 February 2000.

Central banks

In the UK, the central bank is the Bank of England. Unlike other banks whose clients are companies and individuals, it serves British government departments and the commercial banks themselves. The UK's reserves of gold and foreign currency are held there. One of the Bank's key responsibilities is to act as 'lender of last resort'. This means that if any of the commercial banks run into trouble and are unable to return deposits to investors, the Bank steps in to provide the funds. This guarantee is important to make ordinary people trust banks with their savings.

The clearing system

The commercial banks all keep accounts at the Bank of England. During a working day, a running total is kept of how much money customers of Barclays, for example, have promised to customers of HSBC. If, at the end of one particular day, HSBC customers owe more money to Barclays customers than the other way round, Barclays' account at the Bank of England is credited with the amount owing and HSBC's is debited. This avoids countless small transactions (deals) between banks.

Sir Edward George was appointed governor of the Bank of England in 1993 and his five-year term was renewed for a further five years in 1998.

Hyperinflation in 1920s Germany led to bank notes of increasingly high values being produced, such as this 50 million mark note. By 1924, notes for 1m million marks were being issued.

In 1923, children in Germany play with bank notes that inflation has rendered practically worthless.

Managing inflation

A fall in the value of money is known as 'inflation'. (For example, something costing £12 in 1997 could have been bought with just £1 in 1960.) Inflation can happen when the supply of money increases. If more bank notes are printed, but there are still the same amount of goods available, sellers feel tempted to demand more bank notes for their wares. It can also happen if the cost of producing the goods goes up. In this case, the manufacturers will want more money for their product than before.

Another important responsibility of the Bank of England is to maintain the value of money, to stop prices rising too much, so that the UK remains competitive with the rest of the world. The government sets a target for inflation which the Bank has to meet. It does this partly by influencing the price of money (the interest rate). If the interest rate goes up, borrowing money becomes more expensive and there is less available to spend. If the interest rate goes down, borrowing becomes cheaper and there is more money in the economy to enable it to grow. Each month the Bank's Monetary Policy Committee meets to decide what rate to charge its customers, the other banks, who adjust the rates they charge their customers accordingly.

Managing the National Economy

The government aims to maintain and, ideally, to raise the standard of living for the citizens of the United Kingdom. To do this, politicians must manage the economy successfully, in other words, put the resources available to society to the best possible use. These resources include people who can make goods and provide services.

The UK has a mixed economy. This means that some goods and services are provided by the public sector, which the government controls, and others by the private sector, in which individuals take financial risks and hope to gain financial rewards. The Treasury is the government department responsible for coming up with and carrying out the government's policy for managing the nation's finances and the economy in general. The minister for finance is known as the Chancellor of the Exchequer, and is responsible for the Treasury's work.

The Budget
Each spring and autumn, the Treasury presents an economic forecast, known as the Budget. In the Spring Budget, the Chancellor gives a long speech explaining how the government plans to raise funds. The Pre-Budget Report in the autumn then provides a progress report on what has been achieved so far. It also gives an update on the state of the economy and government finances, and sets out the direction of government policy in the run up to the Spring Budget. Government spending plans are announced once every two years at the Spending Review.

The Chancellor of the Exchequer, Gordon Brown, leaving his official residence, Number 11 Downing Street, on Budget Day. In line with a tradition started by W E Gladstone, he carries his papers in a red box. Gordon Brown was appointed Chancellor on 2 May 1997.

'... it is because since 1997 we have put our Labour values and our priorities into action that Britain has greater economic stability, rising investment in health, education and our public services, a national minimum wage for the first time, and the lowest unemployment for a generation.'

The Chancellor of the Exchequer, Gordon Brown, addressing the Labour Party conference on 25 September 2000. The opposition parties might disagree with this assessment (see below)!

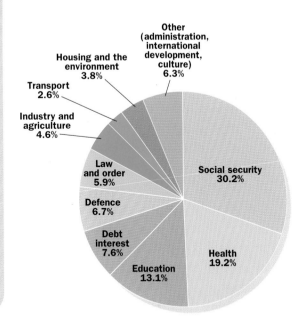

Government spending

The growth of the welfare state during the past sixty years has changed considerably the way in which governments spend their money. In the past, their biggest expenditure was waging war. In 2000-2001, the government dedicated most money to social security (providing welfare such as pensions for old people and unemployment benefit). The second largest piece of the spending pie went to the National Health Service, founded in 1948.

Other important areas of government spending are education, defence, law and order, housing and the environment, industry, agriculture and transport. Spending runs into billions of pounds. Overall, the government spends roughly three-quarters of a million pounds every minute.

This pie chart shows how the UK government divided up its spending in 2000-2001.

'There are serious concerns about the UK economy.... There are concerns that our spending plans outstrip our ability to earn.... It is under this chancellor's governorship that the UK has fallen from ninth to nineteenth in the world competitiveness league.'

Shadow Chancellor Michael Howard, 27 November 2001.

Government funding

To cover the cost of public spending, governments need to raise money. They do this mainly through taxation. Here are some of the ways in which the government imposes taxes:

- Direct taxes, such as income tax and corporation tax, are levied directly on individuals and on companies respectively. Income tax is generally the government's biggest source of revenue. Everyone who earns over a certain amount has to pay it, and the more you earn the more you pay (see opposite).

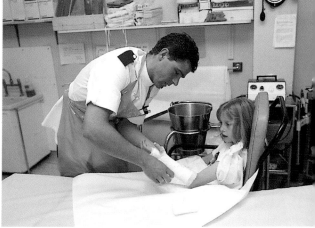

- Indirect taxes are levied on goods and services – so sometimes you don't realize that you are paying them. Value Added Tax (VAT), in particular, is an important source of revenue. It is so called because it is collected at every stage of production of a large proportion of goods and services as value is added to the raw material. In practice, for the consumer, it amounts to a single tax on the final sale price.

The government raises money to pay the wages of public sector employees, such as nurses (above) and teachers.

- Council tax is paid to your local council (not central government) for it to provide local services such as town libraries and refuse collection. Each household pays one bill, calculated according to how much the house or flat is worth and how many adults live there.
- National Insurance is paid to the government by both you and your employer. Paying it entitles you to receive certain benefits in the future, if you qualify for them. These include a state retirement pension, incapacity benefit if you fall ill,

16

jobseeker's allowance if you are unemployed and maternity allowance for women having babies. By the time you are sixteen years old, you should receive your own National Insurance number from the Inland Revenue. You must pay contributions if you are an employed earner between the ages of sixteen and the state pensions age (currently 60 for women and 65 for men), provided you earn more than the lower earnings limit (£72 a week in 2001-2002).

To calculate how much income tax you owe, your income is divided into bands. These and the amount payable can vary from year to year. For example, in the tax year April 2001-April 2002, someone who earned more than the tax-free allowance of £4,535 paid 10 per cent of the extra to the government. This 10 per cent, the 'starting rate', applied to the first band of income up to £1,880. On income more than £1,880 over the allowance (in this case, over £6,415), the person moved into the second band and paid the 'basic rate' of 22 per cent on that additional money. The 'higher rate' of 40 per cent was applied to earners in the third band, with income more than £29,400 over the tax-free allowance.

Paying income tax
The 'tax year' runs from 6 April one year to 5 April the next. Administering tax is the responsibility of the Inland Revenue, under the direction of the Treasury. In the UK, employers operate the Pay As You Earn (PAYE) system, which means that each time they pay you they also pay the right amount of income tax to the Inland Revenue. You then receive your income net (which means the tax has already been deducted) instead of gross (inclusive of tax). This saves you from paying all your tax in one lump sum at the end of the year. If you are self-employed, you must fill out a self-assessment tax return each year, saying how much you've earned.

Protestors opposing the high level of indirect tax on petrol and diesel in autumn 2000.

Borrowing

Governments often spend more than their income. This means they have to borrow to make up the difference. One way they do this is by encouraging members of the general public (often through tax relief) to save their money via the National Savings & Investments scheme. The government can then use that money. Another way is by offering investors Treasury bills, and bonds known as 'gilt-edged securities' or 'gilts'. Like savings accounts, bills and bonds provide investors with income – and gilts are so-called because buyers can be very confident that they will be repaid.

A budget deficit is when government spending is greater than revenue; a budget surplus is when more money is coming in than is going out. The national debt is the amount of money the government owes and it can increase rapidly in times of war. Generally it is never paid off in full, but passed on from generation to generation. The Debt Management Office, part of the Treasury, is responsible for managing the government's debt.

Members of the public can buy products available from National Savings & Investments through any Post Office branch.

The private sector

The UK's Gross Domestic Product (GDP) is the measurement of overall economic activity in the country. It is calculated every quarter (four times a year) by adding up the value of the output of goods and services from businesses. The output from the private sector, those businesses that are run by individuals independently of the government, is far greater than that from the public sector.

A protest march by unemployed workers suffering in the Great Depression of the 1930s.

The government manages the activity of the private sector in an attempt to prevent the country from falling into recession. This is when the level of GDP falls at least twice in a row. When the economy contracts in this way, fewer goods are produced, and unemployment often follows. Millions of people lost their jobs in the 1930s in a terrible world recession, known as the Great Depression.

The government uses money as an essential tool to keep the natural business cycle of 'slump-recovery-boom-recession-slump' from getting out of hand. By controlling the supply of notes and coins and by setting the target for inflation (see page 13), as well as by adjusting taxation rates, it influences how both businesses and consumers behave.

'Although I was keen to make films, I was also particularly attracted by the tax incentives which would enable us to write off the investment against Virgin Music's profits. We produced a number of films... before the tax incentives for making films in Britain were cut.... '
Entrepreneur Richard Branson explaining his period in film-making in his autobiography *Losing my Virginity*.

The UK is part of the global economy. British companies export their products abroad and goods from all over the world are imported for British consumers to buy. Companies often consider it good value to invest and raise money outside the UK and today there are few restrictions to stop them doing so.

London's financial district, known as the City, is a leading world centre for finance and trading and it happens to be in the right place geographically to be able to trade across all the different time zones. Tokyo is hard at work when traders in London arrive early in the morning, Frankfurt, Paris and Zurich then get going and the dealers in New York start work later in the afternoon, London time. Different countries or zones have different currencies. These range from the major ones, including the pound sterling, the US dollar, the Japanese yen and the Euro, to the lesser known Vietnamese Dong.

Exchange rates The exchange rate is the price of one country's currency in terms of another country's currency. If you are going abroad, it determines how much foreign money you will get for your pounds. Sterling has a floating exchange rate, which means it changes constantly. Over the last twenty years, for example, one pound has at some points been able to buy about one US dollar and, at other points, nearly two-and-a-half.

A view of the City of London.

All sorts of things can make the exchange rate vary, or fluctuate. High demand for a currency from investors or low supply from trade can push the rate up, for example. Demand and supply vary according to how well the economy in question is doing. Other considerations, including the country's political stability, may affect the exchange rate.

The Gold Standard

In 1816, the British government adopted the Gold Standard. This meant that sterling was tied to gold – the value of one pound was set to be exactly 123.25 grains of gold. The Bank of England had to exchange paper bank notes for their equivalent worth in gold if requested to do so. (In 1797 it had suspended its commitment to do this because war with France had eaten into its gold reserves.)

The Gold Standard was adopted by most major trading nations during the nineteenth century, including France, Germany, Japan and the US. The effect of this was like fixing exchange rates between the different currencies, because each one was always worth a set amount of gold.

The Gold Standard has been abandoned and re-adopted at several turbulent moments in history. The UK withdrew for good in 1931 and the US finally did the same in 1973. Now most currencies have floating exchange rates, which can change according to market forces.

The threat of a war, for example, may discourage investors. The exchange rate affects prices in world trade; goods can seem more or less expensive to UK importers according to how much the price from the exporting country translates into in sterling.

Foreign exchange market

The foreign exchange market is a network of companies and banks that buy and sell foreign currencies, sometimes with the aid of a broker acting as a middleman between buyer and seller. Companies need to convert foreign currency they have received for goods that they have sold abroad into their domestic currency for use at home. Banks hope to make money by selling and buying different currencies as the exchange rate changes – for example exchanging a large quantity of Euros for dollars when the value of the dollar is low, and then selling the dollars again when their value has increased. The deals often involve huge amounts of money, and the dealer needs to be skilled in picking the best moment to trade. Phone and computer links mean that dealers in centres all over the world can connect up with each other. London is the world's largest foreign exchange centre.

Traders at the largest trading floor in the City at work on the first day of trading of the Euro.

Stock markets

To raise money, certain types of companies, called public limited companies, allow individuals and businesses to buy shares in them. This means the buyer owns a portion of the company. According to what proportion of the overall number of shares in existence a shareholder has, he or she will receive regular payments of a proportion of the company's profits. Holders can sell their shares with the aim of getting more than they paid for them. In the UK, shares are traded on the London Stock Exchange.

Bond markets

Bonds are loans. The borrower, who issues the bond, will return money to the lender, who buys the bond, at an agreed time, and pay an agreed rate of interest until then. Governments and companies issue bonds and they can be re-bought and re-sold many times.

The European currency

The Euro is a new currency. It has replaced the individual currencies of twelve European countries, including Germany, France, Spain, Italy and Ireland. In 1999, exchange rates between the old currencies were fixed. In January 2002, the old money was replaced altogether by Euro bank notes and coins.

Throughout history, politicians and economists have toyed with the idea of a single currency. The idea for the Euro has existed since the European Economic Community, now known as the European Union (EU), was created in 1957. In 1958, the Treaty of Rome outlined the aim of a common European market – to increase economic prosperity and contribute to 'an ever closer union among the peoples of Europe'.

Austria	Schilling
Belgium	Belgian franc
Finland	Markka
France	French franc
Germany	Deutschmark
Greece	Drachma
Ireland	Pound
Italy	Lira
Luxembourg	Lux franc
Portugal	Escudo
Spain	Peseta
The Netherlands	Guilder

The table above shows those EU member states currently participating in the common currency. It also shows the original currency of each country, now replaced by the Euro. Denmark, Sweden and the UK are members of the EU but they do not belong to the single currency at present.

A trader examining his screen. Falling prices are shown in red.

Possible effects of the Euro

There were several motives behind the introduction of the single currency. Supporters argue that the Euro makes it easier for companies in different parts of Europe to do business with each other, in the certainty that exchange rate movements will not affect their profits. It may also make transactions cheaper, as businesses avoid the fees charged by dealers to convert different currencies. Another belief is that, because it is easier to compare prices in one currency, it is simpler now than it was in the past to work out the cheapest place to buy goods.

Opponents of the Euro see some disadvantages. The interest rate (see page 13) is set at the same rate across all the different countries, which means that if it is adjusted to benefit one, for example Portugal, it could have damaging effects in another, say Germany. While in theory any Germans who lost their jobs as a result could move to Portugal to find work, the language barrier would probably prevent them doing so. Another worry for some is that the Euro is managed by the European Central Bank (ECB), based in Frankfurt, Germany. The ECB sets the interest rate, not the central banks of each member country. This means that politicians of individual countries, and the people who elected the politicians, have less control over what happens to the interest rate.

Euro notes.

Around 65 per cent of adults play the National Lottery regularly. A more reliable approach to covering the cost of living is to earn money – by working. From the age of sixteen you are allowed to work full time. Up until the age of sixteen you can only work a set number of hours per week and do certain types of jobs, such as babysitting.

How much you are paid depends on the sector you work in and the job you do within that sector. For example, average weekly earnings for jobs in banking and insurance tend to be higher than those in agriculture and the hotel and restaurant business. Some jobs or sectors pay wages based on an hourly or weekly rate. Others offer a salary, which is a payment generally agreed at an annual rate and paid monthly.

A young man at work in an office. Non-manual workers make up 65 per cent of the work force.

Spending

Marketing campaigns and newspaper, TV and billboard advertisements all encourage you to spend. But before you buy something, you should be sure that it's the right product for you and that you can afford it. Banks are often happy to charge you to spend money you don't have! Handing over a plastic card or typing in a credit card number on a web site can feel dangerously unreal, and not like spending money at all.

Shopping for clothes is one way to spend a lot of money quickly!

As well as responsibilities, consumers have certain rights, called statutory rights. When you buy something, the law says it must meet the standard a reasonable person would regard as acceptable, bearing in mind what it cost and other relevant circumstances. It must also be fit for its purposes and match any description supplied. If these rights are abused, you have a right to your money back or other compensation.

Current accounts

Current accounts are designed for handling the money you use day-to-day and most will provide you with certain tools to do so (see box opposite). Many banks and building societies offer children's accounts for you to open from a certain age. Generally they ask you to switch to an adult account when you reach the age of eighteen.

In order to bank a cheque, the date, amount (in figures and words) and the name of the person being paid must all be filled in – and it must be signed. Any amendments that are made should be initialled.

Saving

Savings accounts don't offer as wide a range of facilities as current accounts, but they generally provide a higher rate of interest. If you keep £100 in an account for a year, a 2 per cent rate of interest would earn you £2 at the end of the year, whereas a 6 per cent rate would bring in £6. With big sums of money and over a long period of time, this difference can add up.

24-hour ATMs (cash machines) are a convenient way to withdraw cash from your bank account whenever you need it.

Current account facilities

Cash card: this allows you to withdraw money from a cash machine by tapping a secret code, called a PIN or Personal Identification Number, into the machine and following the instructions.

Debit card: the shopkeeper swipes this plastic card in a machine, you sign a slip and the money is transferred from your bank account straight away.

Cheque book: cheques are written instructions to your bank, completed and signed by you, to pay a certain amount of money to the person whose name you write on the cheque.

Standing order: this is a regular payment for a fixed amount taken directly from your bank account and credited to the account of the person or company you name when you fill out the instruction form for your bank.

Direct debit: you fill out a form for the company you wish to pay – it could be the phone company for your phone bill, for example – authorizing them to take whatever money you owe them from your account when necessary. The amount might change with each payment.

Investing Investing is not as safe as saving. When you invest money you run the risk of getting back less than you put in, or at worst losing it altogether. However, the returns – the money that your money earns – can be much more significant than those from a bank or building society account.

Many people invest for their retirement via a private or company pension scheme, and this is encouraged through tax relief because the state pension is not a huge amount. The pension manager invests your regular monthly contribution in the markets. The idea is that, by the time your working life ends, there will be enough to pay you a regular income and a lump sum. Obviously the earlier you start contributing to a pension the better. Shares are another form of investment (see page 22): to invest in shares you need quite a large amount of time and money to play with, as well as an understanding of how businesses work.

Borrowing There are several ways to borrow money. One is to take out a loan from one of the many companies that sells them. Another is having an overdraft, a facility offered by many banks where you can spend more money than you have in your account, up to an agreed limit. You pay interest on the borrowed money, and sometimes a fee for the service.

Many students take out cheap loans from the government to help cover the cost of their higher education.

> '**Annual income twenty pounds, annual expenditure nineteen nineteen six, result happiness. Annual income twenty pounds, annual expenditure twenty pounds ought and six, result misery.**'
> The financially-challenged Mr Micawber, a character from the novel *David Copperfield*, written in 1850 by Charles Dickens.

Many banks and other companies offer credit cards. These act like debit cards, except instead of the money coming out of your bank account, you have a period of about a month in which to pay it. If you do not pay the money back in time, you pay a large amount of interest, often in the region of 17 per cent, on the money owed until you do. Credit cards are a very expensive way to borrow.

A mortgage is the biggest debt many ordinary people have in the course of their lives. Mortgages are long-term loans made to house buyers, and are often repayable over a period of twenty-five years. The lender has the right to take the house if payments on the loan are not met.

Many students take out loans to finance their further education. In order not to discourage people too heavily from continuing their studies, the government ensures these loans cost much less than commercial loans.

Managing money, to become its master not its slave, is something both individuals and governments often struggle to get right. But, love it or loathe it, money – in all its constantly changing forms – is something that few people can afford to ignore!

Activity
To achieve happiness rather than misery, it's never too soon to get in the habit of managing your finances. The easiest way is to draw up a personal budget. You need to note down your income and make sure that your expenditure comes in at equal or ideally less. Some income might be regular and dependable, such as from a part-time job or savings account interest, and other irregular and hard to predict, like birthday gifts, which means you can't count on it. Then look at your outgoings. These might divide into toiletries, clothes, travel, food and drink, going out. How much can you afford to spend on these things each week? What else do you spend money on? Is there any left over to save for something special in the future? Try doing this in pairs – be your partner's financial adviser and tell him or her where you think they could save money and where they're being unrealistic about their spending.

Glossary

Budget government fundraising plans, as outlined in an annual speech by the Chancellor

capital money or other assets provided to a business to enable it to function

Central Bank the bank for the government and the banking system – in the UK, the Bank of England

Chancellor of the Exchequer UK minister for finance

corporation tax tax charged on the profits of a company

credit to enter as a positive asset in an account

currency the money of use in a particular country

current account a bank account used for a person's day-to-day affairs

debit to enter as an amount owing in an account

deposit a sum of money left with an organization, such as a bank, for safe-keeping or to earn interest

Economic and Monetary Union (EMU) the process by which countries in the European Union are linked by means of a single currency

Euro the new currency for most of the countries in the European Union

exchange rate the price at which one currency can be exchanged for another

export to send out goods or services for sale in another country

fixed exchange rate an exchange rate that does not vary

floating exchange rate an exchange rate that varies according to market forces

fraud deception in order to gain material advantage

gross domestic product a measurement of overall economic activity in the UK calculated by adding up the value of the output of goods and services from businesses

gross income income before tax has been paid on it

import to bring in goods or services to a country

income tax tax on the money made by an individual

inflation a situation that occurs when prices rise and, as a result, the value of money falls

interest the price of money, for example, the amount a person pays to borrow money or the amount that the banks pay to borrow it

investment the purchase of assets with a view to making money from them

investor a person who makes investments

legal tender money that must be accepted when paying a debt

levy to raise (taxes)

national debt the amount of money the government owes, generally handed down from generation to generation

net income the income that remains after tax has been paid on it

pension an investment designed to give a person an income throughout his or her retirement

public limited company (plc) a company that is entitled to issue shares to the public

profit the gain made when something sells for more than it costs to produce; the rate of return on capital

reserves gold and currencies held at the Central Bank

revenue any form of income

Royal Mint the government department responsible for the manufacture of coins for the UK (and some other countries)

self-assessment tax return a form filled out once a year by the self-employed and by any tax-payers who have more complex tax affairs than the norm – the declaration of income and personal circumstances allows the Inland Revenue to calculate the amount of tax owed to the government

social security government payment of allowances to the sick, unemployed or other people in need

sterling the UK pound (as opposed to pounds in other countries, such as Egypt)

tax relief the right not to pay tax where normally you would expect to pay it

Treasury the government department responsible for financial and economic policy

welfare state the system by which the government undertakes chief responsibility for providing for the social and economic security of its people (through old age pensions, education, healthcare, unemployment benefit, and so on)

Resources

Visits

Visits can be made to the Bank of England Museum, Bartholomew Lane, London EC2R 8AH
http://www.bankofengland.co.uk
Education Group telephone: 020 7601 3985/3833/3339
email: education@bankofengland.co.uk
The museum is free and open Monday-Friday, 10am-5pm. It offers an excellent overview of the history and work of the Bank from its foundation to the present day, with displays of old coins, bank notes and much more. It also offers special educational services.

Information books

What Happens in the Stock Exchange, Soraya Moeng, Franklin Watts, 2000
This book is a good way to help children find out more about how the London Stock Exchange works.
The Pound, David Sinclair, Random House, 2000
The story of the pound from its origins to the present day.
The Money Machine – How the City Works, Philip Coggan, Penguin, fourth edition, 1999
A beautifully clear explanation of the workings of the financial world.

The Sunday newspapers are a useful source of information on personal finance as they provide regular overviews of current deals on savings accounts and investments. The *Financial Times* publishes detailed financial news and information Monday to Friday, and covers personal finance on Saturdays.

The internet

http://www.treasury.gov.uk
The UK Treasury web site
http://www.inlandrevenue.gov.uk
The Inland Revenue (tax affairs) web site
http://www.dss.gov.uk
The Department for Work and Pensions web site
http://www.euro.ecb.int
The official Euro site (European Central Bank)
http://www.ftyourmoney.com
A web site offering personal finance help and advice
http://www.which.net/legal/contents.html
A web site offering consumer rights help and advice
http://www.ncc.org.uk
The web site of the National Consumer Council (an independent body representing the interests of UK consumers of goods and services of all kinds, in both the public and private sectors)
http://www.nationallottery.co.uk
The National Lottery web site

Index

Numbers in **bold** refer to illustrations.

automated teller machines (ATMs) 9, **27**

bank accounts 9, 11, 26-7, 29
Bank Charter Act (1844) 7
bank notes *see* paper money
Bank of England 7-8, 9, 10, **10**, **11**, 12, 13, 21
barter 5, **5**, 6
bonds 23
borrowing 10, 11, 12, 13, 18, 28
Brown, Gordon 14-15, **14**
Budget, the 14
building societies 11, 17, 26, 28

capital 12
cash/credit cards 8, 9, **9**, 11, 26, 27, 29
Chancellor of the Exchequer 14, **14**
cheque books 11, 27
cheques 8
City of London, the 20-21, **20-21**
coins 6, **6**
commercial banks 11, 12
council tax 16
cowrie shells 6, **6**
creditor 8

debit card 27, 29
debt 8
deposits 7, 11, 12
direct debit 27

e-commerce 9
European Central Bank 24
European currency 23, 24, **24**
European Union 23
exchange rate 20-24

foreign exchange market 22
forgery 9

George, Sir Edward **12**
gilt-edged securities 18
goldsmith-bankers 7, 10
Gold Standard 21
government spending 15, **15**
Great Depression, the 19, **19**
Gross Domestic Product (GDP) 18

indirect taxes 16
inflation 13, **13**, 19
Inland Revenue 16, 17
interest 11, 17, 26, 29
interest rate 13, 23, 24
investing 28
investment banks 12

kina shells 6

legal tender 8
loans 28-9

merchant banks *see* investment banks
mortgages 29

national debt 18
National Insurance 16
National Lottery 25
National Savings & Investments Scheme 18

overdrafts 28

PAYE (pay as you earn) 17
paper money 7-8, **7**, **8**, 13
pensions 28

receipts 7
recession 18-19
Royal Mint 6

saving 10, 11, 26
shares 28
standing orders 27
statutory rights 26
stock exchange 12
stock market 22

tax relief 18, 28
taxation 16-17, 19
traders **22**, **23**
Treasury 14, 17, 18
Treaty of Rome (1958) 23

Value Added Tax (VAT) 16

wampum 6
watermark 9